JAPAN

A Photographic Journey

TEXT: **Bill Harris**

DESIGN: **Teddy Hartshorn**

EDITORIAL: **David Gibbon**
Nicola Dent

PRODUCTION: **Ruth Arthur**
Sally Connolly
Neil Randles

DIRECTOR OF PRODUCTION: **Gerald Hughes**

PICTURE SOURCES: **Prisma – Zurich, Switzerland**

JAPAN

A Photographic Journey

Text by
BILL HARRIS

CRESCENT BOOKS
NEW YORK • AVENEL, NEW JERSEY

Visitors to cities that are foreign to them usually get their first taste of the unfamiliar culture from taxi drivers. In London they are predictably polite and knowledgeable. They are friendly in Rome, too, even though their passengers are happy that the cab is equipped with seat belts. New York cabbies are world famous for the opinions they share, and in Paris it is a good idea to have a positive opinion of the driver's dog, who may be sharing the ride. But in Tokyo and other cities in Japan, a trip in a taxi is often an experience that even the most seasoned travelers never quite forget.

As soon as the door is closed the meter starts, and the driver takes off with the kind of start that draws cheers at a Le Mans auto race. Even if driver and passenger understand the same language, neither has spoken yet, but it probably doesn't matter. Unless the destination is a landmark, the driver doesn't know where it is anyway. But finding it is half the fun. It could take an hour or more if he is looking for a private house, and the meter will be counting every second of it.

Westerners visiting Japan look forward to a certain amount of culture shock, a touch of the exotic, the adventure of being a stranger in a strange land. But few of them are prepared for what may be one of Japan's greatest contributions to the inscrutability of the East: the system known as *banchi*. Very few streets anywhere in the country have names, and although some houses have numbers, they refer to age, not location. The first house built in a district is designated number one, but two could be a long distance away and three in a completely different direction. And if more than one house is on the same lot, which is usually the case, they share the same number. The major cities are divided into districts, called *ku*, whose blocks are also numbered, although in no particular order and with the numbers frequently repeated. To add to the confusion, the blocks, known as *chome*, are usually chopped up by nameless alleys packed with houses, possibly including the one the taxi driver is looking for.

But the driver isn't without help. As far as he's concerned, that is what the police are for. Tokyo visitors are usually surprised by the seeming anarchy of the city's traffic patterns as motorists, pedestrians and cyclists seem left to their own devices while police officers stay inside little kiosks politely waiting for one of them to get lost. There are more than 1,200 of the small, street-corner police stations in Tokyo, each with a list of all the residences and businesses in their area. Their occupants are eager to be of service, if for no better reason than to offer proof that banchi is the best of all possible systems for keeping track of real estate in a land where so little of it is divided among so many people.

Mailmen and bill collectors may not agree, but it is a tradition that goes back thousands of years, and no one expects it to change any time soon. Their ancestors invented the system to help them stay out of the sight and minds of evil spirits, and modern Japanese, although not as influenced by the spirit world, are just as pleased to have their privacy reinforced by anonymous housing.

Western visitors usually have a problem making up their minds whether the Japanese culture is unfathomably alien or a slavish imitation of their own ways. Such impressions are understandable when they stand aside on a busy Tokyo street for a procession of priests being pulled in carriages by men with white strips of cloth on their heads so they don't have to waste time mopping their brows; and themselves protected from the sun by servants struggling with huge red parasols. At the same moment, on a bridge over their heads, a bullet train, the super-express the Japanese call *shikansen*, is starting its run toward Kyoto and will soon be speeding along at 130 miles an hour. And while the availability of McDonald's hamburgers in Vienna seems almost ·natural, it sometimes comes as a surprise in Tokyo. No one seriously believes that the Viennese are going to abandon their coffee houses to the lure of Coke and Pepsi, but some visitors on the other side of the world are convinced that such Western tastes will provide another example of the Japanese penchant for imitation, and that sooner or later the tea ceremony will be swallowed up in a sea of soft drinks.

The Japanese are undeniably good imitators, but nearly a century-and-a-half has passed since they opened their doors to the West, and if it brought them blue jeans and pin-striped suits, their own traditions are still very much intact. While they often adapt ideas that suit them, they are just as likely to reject the ones that don't. For instance, when the Americans arrived in 1945 and took charge of things, one of the first things they did was to start naming the streets. The Japanese just smiled. When the occupiers went home seven years later they left behind a new democratic government, but they also left a lot of rusting street signs that no one had even noticed. Despite all those years with Westerners in their midst, the Japanese still preferred to eat in private but bathe in public, and they were willing to insist that women should earn the same salaries as men, but were equally insistent that women still weren't equal to men. And it never occurred to them that the labor-saving devices the Americans taught them to love so much gave them an opportunity to get their work done faster so they could have more time to relax. To the Japanese, a machine simply represents a chance to do more work.

In spite of their reputation as imitators, the Japanese have spent most of their history isolated on their islands, and they are almost unique among the world's peoples for having developed their own culture themselves with few outside influences. But there have been some exceptions.

Chinese historians mention a unified culture in the land they called *Wa*, which seems to have been established in 660 B.C. Japan's own recorded history doesn't begin until the 5th century A.D., about the same time as the fall of the Roman Empire, because it wasn't until then that immigrants from China brought their system of writing, and the Japanese emperors began keeping records and compiling chronicles. The Chinese also brought the teachings of Confucius, which included the idea of family responsibility and the concept of government based on moral character. But the greatest change came from Buddhism, which was introduced by way of Korea at about the same time. The new philosophy complemented the beliefs already established under the umbrella of Shintoism, which placed mankind's existence in the world under the guidance of a variety of gods and spirits known as *Kami*. Eventually, the two religions learned to coexist, but the ideas of the Buddhists weren't welcomed with open arms in the beginning.

Although the philosophy moved the Soga, an important court family, to promote it as the new state religion, not everyone was quite sure it was a good idea. Possibly that was because the Korean king who introduced them to it hadn't mastered the art of persuasion. His formal presentation said that this new doctrine could lead to "a full appreciation of the highest wisdom," but added that "it is hard to explain and hard to comprehend." The idea was also strongly opposed by the powerful Nakatomi clan, which had assumed the responsibility of performing Shinto rituals at court, and by the Mononobe, which represented the military and was suspicious of a religion based on self-knowledge and self-mastery, which they didn't think were very good qualities for a disciplined army. The Soga finally prevailed, but in a way that might have made the Buddha weep.

After suppressing the other factions in a series of bloody intrigues, Soga no Umako, the chief minister, arranged for the assassination of the emperor, who, although his nephew, was a member of the Yamato clan, the traditional ruling family. Then he replaced the ruler with his niece, Suiko, Japan's first empress. Of course, Umako had no intention of letting her have any authority, and appointed her nephew, who became known as Prince Shotoku Taishi, as her Regent. It was his plan to be the power behind the throne, but the Prince Regent, though married to a Soga, was also related to the Yamato clan, and during the nearly fifty years he served, he carefully watched over the interests of the traditional ruling family. Although it wasn't exactly what Umako had in mind, he insisted that all his battling and intrigues had only been to bring the teachings of Buddha to the Japanese court, rather than a grab for personal power. And for that he couldn't have picked a better vehicle than Shotoku Taishi.

The Prince was an ardent Buddhist, and what Constantine accomplished by bringing Christianity to Rome, Shotoku did for Japan, spreading the Buddhist philosophy throughout the country and establishing monasteries and temples at key places, as well as instigating new laws based on Buddhist principles. Although the philosophy had come to Japan from Korea, and had been founded in India, Shotoku associated it with China, and in addition to spreading the religion he also promoted Chinese scientific ideas and encouraged Chinese-style sculpture and painting. His people were as enthusiastic about the new ideas as he was, and through most of the seventh century the Japanese were sorting through the culture of China like a candy-lover with a new box of chocolates, picking what pleased them and discarding what didn't. But nothing pleased them exactly as they found it, and ideas born in China went through a profound transformation as they crossed the Sea of Japan.

The changes also had a dramatic effect on the Japanese political structure. After Shotoku Taishi died, the competing clans began fighting among themselves again, and power soon fell to a coalition of families led by the Nakatomi, who reaffirmed the change in the air by taking the name Fujiwara. The Yamato clan was still the Imperial Family, and its legendary divine origins were enhanced to keep them above the political battles that everyone knew would continue. But after taking control of the court in 645, the Fujiwara became the most powerful family in Japan, and if its political influence rose and fell and rose again, its place at the top of Japanese aristocracy was unquestioned until the aristocracy itself was abolished exactly thirteen centuries later.

The Fujiwara ascendency was marked by *Taikwa*, the Great Reform, that began centralizing the power of the Japanese state. Land was redistributed and became state owned when the owners died. Hereditary titles were abolished, the country was divided into provinces run by court-appointed governors, and the tax structure was completely revised. The islands were even given an official name, *Nippon*, the pronunciation of the two Chinese ideographs that represented the source of the sun. Nearly all the changes Taikwa brought were based on Chinese models, but there were some differences. For instance, the Confucian system of a civil-service bureaucracy filled by means of open examinations became the Japanese standard, but, unlike in China, noble birth was the only route to important government jobs in Nippon.

But if the Japanese were careful to keep their own traditions intact in the midst of reform, the sudden growth of the central government gave them an unexpected problem. Strong among ancient Japanese beliefs was the idea that death polluted the place where it struck, and when an emperor died the entire capital had to be moved to fresh surroundings. No one was quite sure it was a good idea, and faced with the burden of moving the whole bureaucracy every few years, they decided to build a new city and make it their permanent capital. Patterned on the lines of the Chinese Imperial City, the new capital at Nara had one important difference: there was no wall around it. The Japanese didn't like the idea of being cut off from the natural world around them, even if it might leave them open to attack.

At its height Nara was home to more than 200,000 people, and if there was no apparent threat from outside, the concentration of public officials, noble families and powerful monks made it a hotbed of intrigue and conflict from within. The problem was solved in 795, when the Emperor Kwammu moved the government to the brand-new city of Kyoto, leaving the Buddhist priests to go on fighting among themselves in the old capital, while Kyoto became the centerpiece of Imperial Japan for more than a thousand years. Among Kwammu's innovations was the establishment of a university in Kyoto and colleges in each of the provinces. The new emphasis on learning, which was largely restricted to the upper classes, had a profound effect on the flowering of art and culture, but it also had a down side. Of the next thirty-three emperors, nineteen abdicated so that they could spend their time studying rather than dealing with the problems of governing, and the clan leaders, most notably the Fujiwara, were more than happy to fill the power vacuum. It became customary for them to marry their daughters to new emperors, who would willingly abdicate as soon as the bride produced a son. In the process, the mother would become the empress dowager, with her father serving her as regent. At the end of the 9th century, a single regent served as the power behind the thrones of no less than eight different emperors. By then the Japanese decided that they had learned everything the Chinese had to teach them, and at the beginning of the 10th century they isolated themselves from the rest of the world and began to concentrate on refining borrowed ideas into something uniquely their own.

Among the Chinese concepts that didn't take root in Japan was the idea of forced military service. It was tried and found wanting because of the burden it put on farmers, but without a centralized military the provincial aristocrats began forming their own armies, and by the early 10th century they had transformed themselves into a military elite whose power came from the small farmers and land owners who depended on them. They were known as *samurai*, a term meaning "those who serve."

Their skills as fighting men were honed in the Kanto Plain on the east coast of the island of Honshu. Two noble families who were based there, the Minamoto, known as the *Genji*, and the Taira, usually called the *Heiii*, made their names by providing military service to the government. Their warriors also kept in fighting trim defending their lands against frequent attacks from the north. By the beginning of the 12th century, the Minamoto had become dominant at the Imperial court by saving it from attacks by samurai armies serving Buddhist monks. The Taira, meanwhile, secured their authority by fighting pirates on the Inland Sea. They squared off against each other in the 1150s, when they took opposite sides in disputes among the Fujiwara over political appointments and, in the end, they not only substituted military for civilian officers in the government, but also curbed the influence of the Fujiwara in the process. The Taira became the clear winners in their war when the Minamoto chief was killed, but contrary to custom his sons were allowed to live. It was a decision that the Taira chieftain, Kiyomori, would regret.

With the empire firmly in his hands, Kiyomori moved to Kyoto to claim his share of the good life. In time he arranged for his daughter to marry the emperor and, following tradition, his grandson eventually became emperor himself. But the luxuries of court life made Kiyomori soft, and in the meantime the sons of his old enemy were building their strength. The uprising they started lasted five years, and in the end Minamoto Yoritomo was able to establish his own government at Kamakura, which became known as the shogunate after the emperor gave him the title of Seii-tan-Shogun, "the barbarian-subduing Commander-in-Chief." He referred to his rule as *bakufu*, the tent government.

Although powerful, the early shoguns never controlled all of Japan and eventually became little more than figureheads charged with the protection of the emperor, who was himself a figurehead. In time, though, stronger heads and other clans prevailed, and in the early 13th century all power was transferred to Kamakura, and courtly life gave way to a military society that dominated Japan for the next six hundred years. At the same time a religious revival swept through Kamakura in the form of two new Buddhist sects. One, known as *Jodo*, the Pure Land, preached that the world was an evil place and that Nirvana could only be attained after death, which the faithful should spend their lives preparing for. The other was *Zen*, which was brought to Japan in the 7th century, but was hardly noticed until it was resurrected in 1192. It stressed contemplation as the road to Nirvana which, according to its teachings, existed within the soul. Oddly, it was Zen the samurai embraced, even though they were warriors and not usually given to deep thoughts. Zen's appeal was partly based on the idea that every man's destiny was in his own hands and that an austere existence was a major route to salvation. To a samurai it also provided a means of tempting fate on his own terms. The ultimate effect of the new religion was to unite the Japanese as a nation at a time when they needed unity more than ever.

Although they had existed in their own closed world for three centuries, the outside world began threatening them when the great leader of the Mongols, Kublai Khan, became emperor of China in 1259. His grandfather, Genghis Khan, had already overrun

Korea, which meant that the new Chinese empire extended to within fifty miles of Japan. The Mongols obviously wanted to expand into the Japanese islands, but their military power was concentrated in their cavalry, and they needed Korean ships and sailors if an invasion was to be attempted. It made the Japanese feel relatively secure, because their relationship with the Koreans was unusually friendly, but they were unnerved when the Great Khan sent a message to their emperor. It began by pointing out that, "Our ancestors, who have received the Middle Empire by the inscrutable decrees, became known in numerous far-off lands, all of whom have reverenced their power and majesty." After confirming Mongol superiority, the note continued that, "We beg that hereafter you, O King, will establish friendly relations with us so that the sages may make the four seas their home." Then the message ended with a warning that any refusal of friendly overtures might lead to war. "And who is there who likes such a state of things?," asked the man who had pointedly referred to himself as the emperor of Great Mongolia, but addressed the Japanese emperor, a figure descended from the sun itself, as nothing more than a king.

The samurai warriors had developed their skills fighting one another, and they followed rigid rituals that both sides understood and respected. But when the Mongol army landed on their shores, none of the old rules applied. It was the samurai custom to rush at the enemy, single out the toughest-looking among them, and slice off his head, which then became a trophy to wave at the next prospect. The Mongols, on the other hand, had swept through the rest of East Asia fighting in tight, well-disciplined units, which gave them a decided advantage. They also had the advantage of catapults that hurled great flaming iron balls into the enemy's ranks, and although the samurai had what they considered the greatest advantage of all, their incredible bravery, they were forced to retreat behind the walls of an old fortress where, as their historian recorded, they expected to be destroyed to the last man and "that no seeds would be left" to carry on their tradition. What they had no way of knowing was that their fierce tactics had unnerved the Mongols and, spurred by fears that reinforcements were on the way, the invading army retreated to its ships. A typhoon came up as they reached the open sea and most of the ships sank, taking thousands of lives and putting an abrupt end to the first invasion of Japan.

Kublai Khan wrote off the loss as an act of nature, but he had other things on his mind at the time and didn't repeat the attack until seven years later. The delay gave the Japanese time to prepare, with such defenses as a twenty-five-mile wall surrounding Hakata Bay on the island of Kyushu, and heavily-manned garrisons at other places where an attack might be likely. The attack came at Hakata Bay in June, 1281. The wall held and the samurai took advantage of the standoff by raiding the enemy ships, deftly removing the heads of the soldiers crowded below decks. The bloodbath went on for more than six weeks before Mongol reinforcements arrived, and the Japanese knew from experience that the bravery of their warriors wasn't going to save them from the Mongol horde. There was nothing left to do but to pray, and the nation began pleading with its gods for help.

Help came in the form of a tornado that swept through the anchored Mongol fleet and completely destroyed it. The invaders who weren't drowned were dispatched by samurai swords and Japan was saved, thanks to the *kamikaze*, the divine wind. It convinced the Japanese people that their land was, indeed, protected by heaven, and gave them a sense of invincibility that sustained them for centuries. But the heaven-sent victory gave the military government a headache. Although they had won the war, they hadn't claimed any new territory, which was traditionally used as rewards to faithful soldiers, and because they believed that prayer had saved the day, the religious establishment was also pressing for rewards. The situation eventually led to the overthrow of the Kamakura shogunate, but it also led to a series of civil wars that raged for most of the next two centuries.

Trouble began for the warlords when Go-Daigo became emperor in 1318 As was customary, he was asked to abdicate eight years later, but he refused and then insulted his would-be masters by naming his own son as the heir apparent. It was an affront that couldn't go unpunished, and an army of 3,000 men was sent to Kyoto to force him to see the error of his ways. The emperor was sent into exile, but within a few months, with the help of Ashikaga Takauji, the army commander who had been sent to fight him, Go-Daigo was back on his throne.

The emperor, heartened by the support, began to reform the government and restore his own authority, and before long his own army attacked Kamakura. When the battle was over, the Regent, who by tradition had been the country's real ruler, was forced to commit suicide and Go-Daigo emerged as the most powerful emperor in his own right in hundreds of years. But when the time came to reward the men who had made his victory possible, Takauji felt his own reward fell far short of what he believed he deserved. In the meantime, members of the Hojo clan who until then had been running things, retook Kamakura, and Takauji was sent to put the rebels in their place. But, once having accomplished his mission, he established his own shogunate. When his forces attacked Kyoto, Go-Daigo escaped to the south into the hills of Yoshino with all the trappings of his office, but Takauji claimed that by running away he had in effect abdicated, and the new shogun appointed a new emperor.

For the next sixty years Japan had two emperors: one ruling the Northern Court and the other the Southern, and the country was at war with itself. By the time it ended, the Ashikaga Takauji Shogun was the only real power in Japan. The third in the line, Yoshimitsu, who came to power in 1368, reopened the door to China, and the resulting trade brought huge profits that made a cultural renaissance possible. He and his successors built lavish temples and palaces, supported art and literature, and gave the Japanese their passion for landscape gardening and flower arranging, as well as establishing the tradition of the tea ceremony. It was also their influence that helped artisans develop porcelain-making and lacquer work into high art. But in spite of the beauty they encouraged, their country was in an almost constant state of turmoil as farmers rose against their landlords, samurai against their overlords, and warlords battled one another for more power.

In the second half of the 16th century, three powerful military leaders came on the scene and began restoring order. The first of them, Oda Nobunaga, defeated his neighbors for control of an entire province and quickly brought most of central and eastern Japan under his influence. When the shogun was assassinated, his exiled son went to Nobunaga for help, and in return for the success he brought about Nobunaga was rewarded with the title of vice-shogun. Though strong as an individual, Nobunaga also had the advantage of very loyal lieutenants. In his rise as a warrior he had recruited the services of a woodcutter named Toyotomi Hideyoshi, who quickly developed into a brilliant soldier, and he had also impressed another young man, Tokugawa Ieyasu, an overlord with a substantial army of his own. Together they were a formidable combination. As vice-shogun, Nobunaga relied on Hideyoshi's military power to keep his enemies at bay, and on Ieyasu's diplomatic skills to keep the stronger feudal lords quiet. In the meantime, the shogun himself was plotting against Nobunaga, and when he was deposed for his trouble, Nobunaga consolidated all the power into his own hands. He used it to crush the Buddhist priests who had been waging war from their fortified monasteries, and in the process brought peace to huge sections of the country. But his rule came to an end because of a trifling insult to one of his generals, who assassinated him after being hit on the head with a fan. The general immediately proclaimed himself shogun, but he hadn't reckoned with Hideyoshi, who was off fighting a war for his master. When word of the murder reached him, he broke off the battle and rushed back to Kyoto, where he killed the assassin and his minions and nominated Nobunaga's grandson to succeed him. Although it led to problems with the dead shogun's sons, who felt the honor should have gone to them, the two generals, Hideyoshi and Ieyasu, joined forces and went to work to unify their country. Control of all of Japan finally fell to Hideyoshi who, although he had been born a commoner, attained the status of a noble, required of a shogun, by prevailing on the Fujiwara family to adopt him.

But the role of master of his own country wasn't enough for Hideyoshi. He decided to extend the empire, and in 1592 he attacked Korea as the first step in a grand plan to conquer China, and eventually to extend Japanese influence into India. His skills as a general served him well, and in a few weeks the entire Korean peninsula was his. But the seas around it weren't, and in the same few weeks the Korean Admiral Y-Sun unveiled an iron-clad warship – the first in the world – that made short work of the Japanese ships by ramming them and sending them to the sea bottom. Hideyoshi's land forces, meanwhile, were not only cut off from reinforcements and supplies, but also found themselves in unfamiliar mountains at the mercy of unfamiliar winter winds. To make matters worse, Chinese troops suddenly poured down on them from the north and forced them to give up all the territory they had gained. Still Hideyoshi couldn't accept defeat, and four years later he ordered a second attack. This time the Koreans and Chinese were ready for them and the Japanese troops were driven back. But their decision to go home wasn't based on the prospect of defeat – surrender wasn't in the Japanese vocabulary – but was due to the news that their general, Hideyoshi, was dead.

After more bloody internal battles, the government came under the control of Tokugawa Ieyasu, who already owned vast estates including the fortified city of Edo, which he made the head-quarters of his new Tokugawa shogunate in 1603. In order to ensure his power, the new shogun required that the nobles establish their residences surrounding his palace, and ordered that when they left home they should leave their families behind as hostages. The presence of so many influential people made Edo, which years later became known as Tokyo, the Eastern capital, far more important than the Imperial City of Kyoto. Its business community thrived as well, quickly making it more important than Osaka, the country's commercial center, and in less than two centuries, with a population of more than a million, it had become the second-largest city in the world after London.

Ieyasu was interested in promoting foreign trade, but he had a natural suspicion of outsiders. Throughout most of Japan's history, the only outsiders they knew existed were those on the nearby Asian mainland. But sixty years before Ieyasu became shogun, the Western world had intruded on them in the form of a shipwreck. In 1543, three Portuguese attempting to maneuver a Chinese junk, were blown ashore on the island of Kyushu and, after going back to their base at Macao with tales of riches and friendliness, Portuguese merchants began retracing their steps. Five years later, Francis Xavier, the founder of the Jesuit order, arrived looking for converts. He found a few, but his goal was to make a Christian of the emperor himself, and he therefore set off on foot in the direction of Kyoto, three hundred miles away. But he had the misfortune of arriving in the midst of the civil wars, and found both the emperor and the shogun little more than figureheads. He would still have been pleased to baptize them, but after his long walk across Japan, the man who would one day become a Christian saint cut a rather sorry figure. Even though he had letters of introduction from the Pope in Rome, no one in Kyoto had ever heard of the former and couldn't find the latter on a map.

Undaunted by the rebuff, Francis Xavier went back to the Portuguese settlement on Kyushu and changed his image. Outfitted in the clothes of a noble, he gathered together gifts from India and set out again, this time to convert influential local leaders. He kept at it for more than two years before leaving for more fertile ground, but he left behind a tolerance among the Japanese lords, and within twenty years Jesuit priests were welcomed at the Imperial Court.

But it wasn't their religion that made them welcome. The nobles were impressed by the way the Portuguese traders respected the priests, and decided that if they were on good terms with the clerics, the foreign ships were more likely to call at their harbors. The most apparent proof that they were right was the growth of the port of Nagasaki, which had been transformed from a fishing village into one of the richest cities in Japan when the majority of its citizens converted to Christianity.

But the teachings of the missionaries proved a two-edged sword. Believing that theirs was the one, true religion, the Jesuits weren't above putting down the Buddhists and Shintoists, and their more zealous converts followed their lead. To make matters worse, the new Christians were also told that Jesus was the King of Kings and more powerful than shogun and emperor combined. This was at a time when the Shogun Hideyoshi was trying to reunite the country and, finding this Christian God a nuisance, he displayed his own power by ordering the Jesuits to leave the country. It was a decision he himself was unsure of, because he was afraid that if the missionaries left they would take the merchants with them, and he didn't press the point. But he thought he had an ace in the hole. He had learned that Spanish control of the Philippines was shaky, and he offered his services as a protector to the governor of the islands in exchange for trading rights. A whole year went by before he got a reply, and then it was in the form of a delegation of Franciscan missionaries. But Hideyoshi needed the business and he allowed the Spanish to try to convert his people. The Spanish missionaries arrived in force, much to the consternation of the Jesuits, but the Portugese traders didn't follow the missionaries as Hideyoshi had hoped. Hideyoshi tried to put an end to the fighting between the two Christian groups by executing a half-dozen priests and many of their followers, and a few years later his successor, Ieyasu, issued an order that all Japanese Christians should renounce the religion or be put to death. The policy back-fired because it created martyrs, which the Catholic missionaries hailed as the ultimate test of faith. But it is an ill wind that blows nobody any good, and in 1600 the wind brought a Dutch ship piloted by an Englishman named Will Adams. If the Spanish and Portuguese couldn't agree on anything else, they were brought together by the presence of a hated Protestant, and they petitioned the court to have the man executed as a pirate.

Ieyasu wasn't so sure the charge was true, and after personally interviewing the Englishman, the shogun not only spared his life but got Adams to teach him the arts of shipbuilding and seaman-ship. Eventually, Adams was raised to the rank of samurai, with an estate of his own and a Japanese wife, and he was put in charge of dealing with the Dutch and English merchants who were beginning to discover the advantages of calling at Japanese ports. With Adams' help the Japanese also began building a merchant fleet of their own, and their ships ranged all over the Pacific area, even reopening trade with China which had been closed to them for more than one hundred and sixty years.

Their new command of the sea allowed the Japanese to take control of other territories, and in 1630 a delegation was sent to the Philippines to have a look around. Although theoretically locked in their own islands, the Japanese court had a good understanding of what was going on in the world, and they had perceived a pattern among the Spanish and Portuguese to send missionaries to foreign lands to pave the way for conquering armies. Convinced that the Philippines were to serve as a staging ground for a Spanish attack on them, they were determined to invade first. But when the time came cooler heads prevailed, and rather than going off to war, persecution of Christians within Japan was intensified as a means of preventing an invasion by Spanish soldiers. Then, in an attempt to prevent any further outside influence, an order was issued in 1636 forbidding any Japanese citizen to leave the country, and any already abroad, including sailors on ships at sea, were prevented from returning. The penalty in either case was death. The following year the death penalty was extended to include all Christians who refused to renounce their faith.

The edict started an uprising in the Nagasaki area, but after a three-month siege, Dutch ships, forced into action by the Japanese authorities, brought about a surrender after slaughtering 30,000 rebellious Christians. The massacre was followed by the expulsion of the Portuguese, and Japan was then completely cut off from the world for more than two centuries. The only exception were the Dutch, who were rewarded for their anti-Christian service and allowed to stay. But they were confined to an offshore island and were only allowed to leave it once a year to bring gifts to the shogun. Only one ship a year was allowed to bring cargo in from Holland, and with it came Japan's only knowledge of what was happening beyond its shores. The industrial revolution, and other 17th- and 18th-century developments in science and medicine, were therefore completely unknown in Japan. Their self-imposed seclusion also kept the Japanese from expanding their territories in an era when all of the great powers in the West were scrambling to build colonial empires.

But the years of seclusion were far from a dark age in the Land of the Rising Sun. The arts flourished and began reflecting purely Japanese ideas for the first time. And peace, which had been elusive for so many generations, gave everyone a better life. Almost everyone, that is. Over the years a class structure had been established in the military-oriented society, with the samurai at the top of a well-ordered pyramid. Their power included the right to kill or maim anyone beneath them – which was almost everyone – who insulted them in any way. But among their traditions was a rule forbidding them to work to earn money. With no wars to fight, and no rebellions to put down, most of them were poverty-stricken, and many were forced to swallow their pride and turn to money-lenders in the merchant class, down at the bottom of the social scale. Some samurai even became merchants themselves, and over the years the capitalist class became dominant as patrons of the arts and the source of funds for the shogun, the Imperial Court, and the provincial nobles.

At the beginning of the 18th century, the Japanese authorities began allowing their scholars to study books brought from Europe by the Dutch, and although they realized that the world was passing them by, they were still resolved not to rejoin it. Their resolve was dramatized a century later when a British warship arrived at Nagasaki with a request for water and supplies. Realizing that it wasn't an invasion but a request for help, the local governor granted it, but then immediately committed *hara-kiri* in shame. When the shogun heard of the incident he ordered all the officials in the port city to do the same. But such things didn't deter the foreigners. A few years earlier the Russians had dispatched a trade mission that was unceremoniously sent packing, ships of other countries began arriving with similar results, the Russians them-se ves never stopping to try to open the door.

The country that eventually succeeded, the United States, didn't even exist when the door was slammed shut. But by the mid-19th century it had become a power in the Pacific area through its whaling ships, and was determined to be allowed to open Japanese ports as supply bases for itself. The first mission was sent in 1837 but, like all the others, the Americans were driven off. Sixteen years later another delegation arrived in the form of four warships commanded by Commodore Matthew Perry. His show of force made the point, and officials allowed him to land with a letter to the emperor from his commander-in-chief, President Millard Fillmore. The letter asked for the right for American ships to call at Japanese ports, but it was a request, not a demand, and Perry said that he would leave immediately and come back a year later for the emperor's answer. What he didn't know, of course, was that Emperor Komei was not in charge of the country; the Tokugawa Shogun was. Not long after Perry's ships sailed away the shogun died, and in the midst of the confusion, it was decided to send copies of Fillmore's letter to some seven hundred nobles and officials, including the Imperial Court, for advice. The consensus was that war was unthinkable, but that the request of the barbarians should be rejected with contempt.

When Perry came back in 1853, with eight warships, it became obvious to everyone that they couldn't have it both ways and, reluctantly, the Japanese signed a treaty that allowed American ships to call at two ports, Hakodate and Shimoda, and before spring turned to summer similar treaties were negotiated with the Netherlands, Britain, France and Russia. They ended Japan's isolation, but they also began a struggle for power that eventually led to the downfall of the shogunate. Commercial treaties that followed were all signed by the shogun, whom the foreigners had begun to call the Tycoon, and the factions opposed to what they called the Red-Haired barbarians began saying that no treaty was legal without the approval of the emperor, who had not been consulted. Ii Naosuke, a pro-Western noble, engineered the appointment of the eight-year-old Iemochi as shogun, and then began executing or exiling men who opposed him. He himself was eventually assassinated, and his removal from the scene tipped the balance in favor of the *Sonno Joi*, a movement among young samurai dedicated to "revering the emperor and repelling the barbarians."

Meanwhile, the foreigners were establishing themselves in Japan completely unaware of what was going on. They began to get the message, however, as their fellow Westerners were murdered and their enclaves attacked. Attempts to stop the attacks brought foreign troops to Japan, and the shogun's inability to put a halt to the murders forced the emperor to call him to Kyoto to be reprimanded, an action that had been unthinkable for hundreds of years. Another civil war erupted, but in the space of six months both the emperor and the shogun died, in what could be interpreted as divine intervention almost in a class with the kamikaze itself. Within a year the new shogun, Keiki, abolished his office after restoring the emperor's authority, and the fifteen year-old Emperor Mutsuhito declared that a new era had arrived, and its name was *Meiji*, meaning "Enlightened Government." The emperor, who himself took the name Meiji, then moved his capital from Kyoto to Tokyo and began steering Japan into the modern world.

Meiji abolished feudalism and with it the power of the samurai. It did away with class distinctions and established representative assemblies that called for the participation of all classes. The new emperor also reaffirmed the treaties with the foreign powers and announced that he intended to send "learning missions" abroad to bring back ideas from the West on everything from education and government to manufacturing and business. In the 1860s and '70s, the Restoration had produced a telephone and telegraph network, started the construction of railroads, begun a postal service, and established a university at Tokyo as well as compulsory education of all Japanese children. With the help of experts from abroad, the Japanese were also building factories and shipyards and developing a modern army and navy. Ironically, Meiji's most loyal supporters were the ones who had rushed to support the Imperial authority in the hope of driving the barbarians out.

In the 1890s Japan went to war with, and defeated, China; and a few years later drove the Russians out of Korea, the first defeat of a European power by an Asian nation. The victories, combined with an alliance with Britain, finally made Japan a world power in its own right. By 1890 it had developed a new constitution and a government of elected representatives in a parliament called the *Diet*. All in all, it added up to a dramatic leap forward for a country that only fifty years earlier was a collection of feudal estates completely cut off from the outside world. But some old ideas still persisted. Although Emperor Meiji had become a constitutional monarch his powers were still absolute, because the constitution specifically called him "sacred and inviolable." The Meiji era ended with the emperor's death in 1912, and his successor, Yoshihito, took over a unified nation that was still growing and had earned the admiration and respect of the rest of the world. But the world itself was beginning to change. With the acquisition of territory beyond its borders, such as Taiwan and part of Manchuria, Japan had become an empire in fact as well as in name, but in Europe, World War I and the Russian Revolution made "empire" a dirty word. In spite of this, at the end of the war Japan was among the big powers represented at the Versailles Peace Conference and became a member of the League of Nations. In the 1919 negotiations she acquired Germany's former colonies in China, as well as a mandate over its islands in the Pacific, expanding the empire even more at a time when the European empires, with Japan's help, were being broken up.

In the 1930s, when the worldwide economic depression brought the Japanese to near-starvation, nationalistic conservatives began calling for a turn away from Western-inspired traits they characterized as greedy, assertive individualism. It was time, they said, for the country to return to traditional Japanese ideals, including the state-as-family and self-sacrifice in the service of the emperor. The vehicle they claimed would bring it all about was aggression abroad, not exactly a historical Japanese tradition, but one that appealed to an island nation with a growing population. The militarists made their first move in 1928, with clandestine activities in Manchuria that they hoped would goad the Chinese to declare war and give them an opportunity to cast themselves as saviors. The first attempt didn't work, but in 1931 they tried again, and this time they were more aggressive about it. After their agents destroyed a section of the Manchurian railway, the Japanese blamed Chinese saboteurs and marched in to root out the perpetrators, seizing the provincial capital of Mukden (now called Shenyang). Four months later, claiming that the Chinese were harassing them in Manchuria, Japanese troops attacked Shanghai and, after a truce was negotiated, set up their own puppet state of Manchukuo, which remained a part of the Japanese Empire until 1945. The attack, which included bombing densely populated sections of the city, turned world opinion against the Japanese and forced them to resign from the League of Nations, with the result that Japan became a kind of outlaw nation. In May 1932, Prime Minister Inukai Tsuyoshi was assassinated and replaced by military men who confirmed Japanese control of Manchukuo and began moves to use it as a base for a projected attack on the Soviet Union. In the meantime, Japan's new isolation and its successes in China began another wave of super-patriotism. It was characterized by a rush to rid the country of "dangerous thought," and a return to "Japanism," which included rioting and the killing of intellectuals, communists and others who didn't follow the new line. Rather than fighting back, the civilian government gave in to the military in the hope of ending the violence. The result was an increase in the defense budget, a new surge of flag-waving patriotism and a new mood that war was the only means of curing all the country's ills.

The militarists responded with an all-out war against China that began at Beijing (then called Beiping) in July 1937. Two years later, while still fighting in China, the Japanese took on the Soviets in Eastern Mongolia. Badly mauled, and with the loss of 80,000 troops, they switched their emphasis to southern China and Southeast Asia in what the Japanese Prime Minister called a drive to build the "Greater East Asia Co-prosperity Sphere." The translation, of course, was Japanese political and economic control of a new, expanded empire free of Western influence.

In 1940 Japan joined the Axis Alliance between Germany and Italy, and a year later it signed a neutrality pact with the Soviet Union. In the meantime, the civilian government was negotiating a treaty with the American government, but, in October 1941, army minister Tojo Hideki abruptly ended the talks, and two months later a decision was made to provoke a war of "self defense and self preservation" with an air attack on the U.S. naval base at Pearl Harbor in the Hawaiian Islands.

In spite of early successes the tide eventually turned against Japan, and in early 1943 a peace movement began to develop. Tojo was forced to step down and neutral governments were asked to help negotiate an armistice, but the Americans responded that they would accept nothing short of unconditional surrender and the war dragged on. Finally, after an atomic bomb destroyed Hiroshima on August 6, 1945, and a second was dropped on Nagasaki two days later, Emperor Hirohito called on his people to "endure the unendurable" and accept the American terms. The surrender, which was formalized on September 2, 1945, called for an allied occupation of Japan and the end of Japanese sovereignty over any possessions beyond its four main islands. It also demanded that the Japanese military machine should be destroyed and not rebuilt, and the removal of more than 180,000 officials from their positions, twenty-five of whom were convicted of war crimes, for which seven were executed, including Tojo. Shintoism, which had become the state religion, was reduced to equal status with other beliefs and the emperor was forced to renounce his claims of divinity. The new military government was headed by the American General Douglas MacArthur, who rewrote the Meiji Constitution to give more direct power to the people themselves than the Japanese had ever known. Although it began with the words "We, the Japanese people ...," echoing the preamble to the American Constitution, it gave them a British-style cabinet responsible to the voters. The new basic law, which gave voting rights to all adults – women as well as men – over the age of twenty, reconstructed the Diet into two houses, both elected by the people, and it also changed local government from appointed to elected officials. Basic human rights were also guaranteed, and the rights of other countries were protected by a clause forbidding the rebuilding of a war machine, except for a small defensive force.

Japanese recovery in the postwar years amazed the whole world, although the world had been shown what Japanese determination could accomplish a century earlier. Even though the American occupation lasted until 1952, the Japanese were running their own government as early as 1947, and the Americans began concentrating on helping to rebuild the Japanese economy. But well over half the U.S. aid was food, and by the mid-1950s Japan not only didn't need any more help, but also was ready to start helping other recovering nations. By the 1970s Japan ranked second in the world in Gross National Product, a measure of a country's wealth arrived at by combining the Gross Domestic Product, the total value of goods and services produced, with income from overseas investments. In the decade of the 1980s Japan became number one in the world in per capita GNP, with an increase from $8,900 to $23,616.

It didn't happen by accident. At the end of World War II almost all the gains Japan had made since industrialization had vanished. More than forty percent of its factories and transportation network were gone, but it was a blessing in disguise, because all of it was replaced with brand-new, modern facilities. Thanks to their passion for learning, the Japanese already had the world's highest literacy rate, and the work force was not only educated, but well disciplined in the Confucian values of their ancestors, which made them an unusually effective work force. Many of them had gained valuable business experience during the Meiji period, but large numbers of the men who had risen through the ranks of industry were driven out of companies because of their participation in the war effort, leaving the door open for younger, and in some ways more aggressive, management. But most of the traditions established at the turn of the century continued to guide them. They were, after all, age-old ideas that had been guiding Japan from the start. The management structure of the country's first industrial companies was based on the rules of life followed by the samurai, many of whom went on to become captains of industry themselves. The roving knights of medieval Japan wore coats of arms identifying the liege lord they served, and when they transferred their loyalty to corporations they changed their costume, but still continued wearing badges as an outward sign of lifelong fealty. Japanese executives in the 1990s still follow the tradition by wearing pins that identify the corporate family they serve.

During the years of Japan's first Western-style industrialization, the government had established itself as a partner in business enterprises. But it was a silent partner, providing such things as tax incentives and the funding of plants and equipment, making it a point to help business to thrive without actually becoming a part of it. The practices were refined in the postwar years, and although entrepreneurism is the key to the Japanese economic miracle, the government is still working in the background to make sure that every segment of the economy is singing from the same songbook. The traditional Japanese belief in family pride, and the concept of the nation-as-family, makes the most powerful corporate executive, as well as the man who sweeps the floor in a factory, work as hard for the pride of his country as for personal gain or the profits of the company.

The attitude is pervasive, and the entire business community, from producers of silk thread to manufacturers of automobiles, is ready to adapt together as conditions change. The most dramatic example came in the 1970s, when the world's supply of oil went down and prices went up. The Japanese, who have no oil reserves of their own and are completely dependent on foreign sources, weathered the storm, but when it was over they set out to minimize their dependence. Changing their ways required new, expensive equipment, but if it meant reduced profits for a few years, it also meant long-term survival. And to a nation that had spent its entire history in fear of being overrun by outsiders, survival meant gaining status at the top of the world economy.

They needed to conserve expensive energy, and they all agreed on the necessity of improving on new developments in semiconductors and microcircuits that would make their factories more productive. In the process they discovered a whole new industry, and quickly became the world's leading producer of electronics. It may have happened anyway, but the 1973 oil crisis made it happen sooner, and when petroleum prices went up again six years later, Japan was the only industrialized country that escaped the stranglehold of double-digit inflation.

The Western world has taken to studying the Japanese business style with all the fascination of the Japanese who were studying them a century ago. But most of the studies are based on the big corporations, in spite of the fact that about half the Japanese workforce is employed by some four million companies owned by single individuals. On the other hand, most of the Japanese themselves are fascinated by the giants, because they are the ones everyone wants to work for. Only a few succeed. In order even to think of applying for a job in a big corporation, a youngster has to begin in the earliest years of school to qualify for admission to one of the top thirty colleges and universities. Without a quality education, a young person is doomed to work for a small firm at a lower salary, with fewer benefits and far less prestige. But, unlike in Western countries, a young Japanese student rarely thinks of getting an edge by going on to graduate school, and there are almost no courses in business that might help anyway. Japanese corporations much prefer recruits they can train themselves and bring up in their own philosophy, unsullied by ideas gathered in some ivory tower.

Prospects are hand-picked from the late-winter graduating classes in the preferred colleges, and the entire quota starts work on April 1, not a day sooner and not a day later. By October 1, some will have been cast aside, but those who are allowed to stay with the company will have a job until it is time to retire. No one is ever hired for a specific job, and the first few years of a corporate career are spent working as trainees for short periods of time in each of the company's divisions. At the end of the training period the junior executive will know every facet of the company, and the company itself will have a good idea of the employee's character, attitude and intelligence. Promotion is automatic and is based strictly on seniority, with pay raises coming with the same automatic frequency. By the time a group reaches retirement age, everyone in it will be at the same general salary level, no matter what the level of authority, a practice the Japanese feel prevents jealousy and enhances the family relationship between a company and its executives. Compensation is usually low because most corporations prefer to use profits to build the company and not its executives' lifestyle, but a loyal employee can usually count on such benefits as low-cost loans for housing and transportation, regular cash bonuses and low-cost vacations. The vacation benefit is usually left unused, however. The average Japanese worker is allowed fifteen days of paid vacation a year, but few ever take more than seven. In industry, Japanese employees work an average of 2,150 hours a year, compared to 1,924 in the United States.

But if the people are working long and hard, their machines are working even harder. In 1991 the Toyota Corporation unveiled a new plant that turns out long lines of its luxury car, the Lexus. The building is a beehive of activity, with machines clanking and whirring, but there are very few people inside. The only ones, in fact, are the handful of human workers who tend to the needs of the robots that actually assemble the cars, and the people who drive the new cars off the end of the assembly line and onto the ships that will carry them to dealers in the United States and elsewhere.

Such things are a sore point in places like Detroit, and Americans aren't quite sure whether they admire the Japanese as innovators or despise them as rivals. Americans like the idea of being number one in the world, and if they feel threatened, it is only natural. On the other hand, the consensus among the Japanese, at least until now, has been that the Americans represent the only country in the world that has ever proven superiority over them, and they were willing to be fatalistic about it. They are good customers, after all. But in the 1990s, in spite of talk of corruption, a decline in the value of their investments and all the other ills of an economic recession, the Japanese seem to be on the verge of becoming the indisputable number one manufacturing nation in the world. In the view of Confucius, whose beliefs are at the heart of Japanese thought, the world is built on hierarchies, and there can only be one number one. On the other hand, as one of the early Catholic missionaries reported, "it seems that they deliberately try to be unlike any other people." Only time will tell whether they will be content to be just "unlike" their friends the Americans, or if they will feel a need to emulate them by waving a flag in the air and shouting, "We are number one!"

Previous page: Japanese fans decorated with the national flag motif. Right: the ornate castle that forms the main attraction of Matsumoto, in central Honshu. Built on a high plateau amid the Japan Alps, this black-walled stronghold, aptly named Karasujo, or Crow Castle, is often considered one of the country's finest. To the north of Honshu, around Tohoku, stretches the stunning coastline of Matsushima, with its many oddly-shaped islands scattered in Matsu-shimawan Bay (overleaf), an area considered one of the three great scenic wonders of Japan.

A popular day's visit from Tokyo, Nikko is renowned for the magnificence of its temples, especially the Toshogu Shrine (right) which, unusual for Japanese art, is ornately decorated with detailed carvings, paintings, red lacquer and gold leaf. Dating from the early 1600s, the Toshogu Shrine was constructed as a memorial to the mighty warlord, Ieyasu Tokugawa, by his grandson. It took about two years to complete, involving some 15,000 craftsmen from throughout Japan. Overleaf: the lovely Chuzenji Lake, another favorite attraction near Nikko.

Close to Tokyo, and Japan's capital from 1192 to 1333, the peaceful city of Kamakura has remained virtually untouched by the country's turbulent past. Among the city's many Shinto shrines and some sixty-five Buddhist temples is the striking Daibutsu, or Great Buddha statue (left). This giant bronze figure has stood exposed to the elements since the late 1400s, when the building that housed it was washed away.

Developed during the 1870s, Ginza (right) remains one of the best-known and more exclusive of Tokyo's shopping districts. Once consisting of long, willow-lined avenues, the streets are now packed with large stores, boutiques and art galleries which continue to draw crowds despite the many rival locations – including Shibuya (overleaf) – that have since developed.

Crowded by day, Tokyo's bustling streets burst into colorful life by night, when dazzling neon signs illuminate Shibuya (facing page bottom) and Ginza (facing page top, above and overleaf), two of Tokyo's extensive shopping areas. Along with Mexico City and Shanghai, this exhilarating megalopolis is one of the world's largest cities in both area and population.

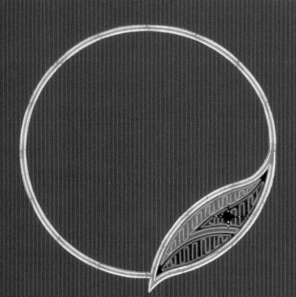

アイスターグループ

アイレディース化粧品

札幌アイスター
東京アイスター
神奈川アイスター
京都アイスター
福岡アイスター

elsa

松山設計

OMRON
マイコン・ベース銀座

ARC Inc.

LUW

AZ INC.

SOW

ユニゾン

micomBASE GINZA

コージーコーナー

COZY CORNER

The lively district of Shibuya (right) grew as a result of the migration that followed Tokyo's Great Kanto Earthquake in 1923, and has since developed as Tokyo's primary entertainment and amusement area. Overleaf: brilliantly colored advertisements – a typical city sight!

The commercial heart of Japan, Tokyo also offers a range of exciting cultural entertainment.
A popular evening out is to go to the opera (facing page bottom), or to visit the spectacular
Takarazuka Review (facing page top). Originating in Takarazuka, this musical extravaganza
has an all-female cast and entails colorful, Broadway-style performances. Equally fascinating
is sumo, or Japanese wrestling (above), often considered the country's national sport. Although
its rules are simple, sumo involves complicated purification rituals at the start of the contest.

A city of contrasts, Tokyo is a blend of old and new. In recent years Japan's vibrant capital has spread both upward and outward, and today's soaring skyscrapers (left and overleaf) – often some fifty stories high – tower over small, low-level buildings. These one- or two-story houses, once a common sight in the city, are rapidly being replaced by their taller neighbors.

Probably the most stunning view of Tokyo is after sundown, when millions of city lights and illuminated signs make this dynamic capital one of the most colorful cities in the world. A maze of brilliantly lit thoroughfares wind through Ginza (facing page), Shinjuku (above) and Shibuya (overleaf), three of the fascinating areas that have developed within Greater Tokyo.

Tokyo's lively entertainment district, Kabukicho (right) is crowded with nightclubs, bars, restaurants, discos, and theaters. Located within the exciting district of Shinjuku, this invigorating subdistrict is a fun place to visit, offering a wide range of evening entertainment from the conservative to the risqué.

High-rise buildings were once a rare sight in Tokyo due to the risk of earthquake damage, but today's soaring towers (these pages) withstand even severe tremors. Both modern offices and apartment blocks have been constructed ever taller, to accommodate the city's thriving business world and the rapidly increasing population. Facing page: Shinjuku. Above: the financial district, and (overleaf) Tokyo Sanyo Securities.

In the days when Tokyo was known as Edo, Ginza (right) was considered the commercial heart of the country. Japan's powerful Ieyasu Tokugawa originally reclaimed the area from swampland, and it was here that he began minting his own silver coins in the early 1600s – "Ginza" means "Silver Mint" in Japanese. Western culture has very much influenced Ginza during its development, and this is particularly evident today. Overleaf: the chic Shibuya district.

Owing to the city's dramatic population
explosion, as well as the devastation caused
by the Great Kanto Earthquake of 1923 and
during World War II, Tokyo has fewer trees
and parks than any other major city in the
world. However, a number of wealthy families
have donated their gardens to public use,
and these include Rikugien Garden (left),
given by Baron Iwasaki, and the 145-acre
Shinjuku Gyoen Park (overleaf), which
once belonged to Lord Naito.

Japan's best-known landmark, majestic, snow-capped Mt. Fuji (above) is viewed from the largest of the five lakes to its north — Yamanaka (facing page top), and from Suruga Bay (facing page bottom), to its south, and dominates the city of Fuji-Yoshida (overleaf). Referred to in reverence as Fuji-san, and often mysteriously shrouded in cloud, this mighty volcano last erupted in 1707. Each year more than a million people make the climb to Fujiyama's summit, with night ascents increasing in popularity.

*Many visitors, both from Japan and overseas, are attracted by the wealth of impressive and
historical buildings – often faithful reproductions of their originals – that are scattered
throughout the country. Nara, in central Honshu, boasts the 8th-century Kasuga Taisha Shrine
(facing page top), its approach lined with 2,000 stone lanterns that are lit at special festivals.
Nara is also home to the world's largest wooden hall, the Daibutsuden (facing page bottom),
which comprises part of the Todaiji Temple complex in Nara-Koen Park, and houses a statue of
the Great Buddha. Nagoya, also in central Honshu, features an attraction of a different kind –
the grand Nagoya Castle (above), with two gilded dolphins adorning the roof. Rebuilt in 1959,
the castle's interior now houses a museum known for its exhibits of armor and weaponry.*

The nation's capital for over 1,000 years, Kyoto (right) is the only one of Japan's major cities to have escaped devastation during World War II, and is a fine blend of traditional culture, art, and architecture. Despite being one of the country's major industrial centers, the city contains many museums, temples and gardens, and attracts some ten million tourists each year.

86

Kyoto is home to over 2,000 temples and shrines, among them the Heian Shrine (above), constructed to commemorate Kyoto's 1,100th anniversary, the Fushimi-Inari Taisha Shrine (facing page top), dedicated to the goddesses of rice and saké, and the splendid Kiyomizu Temple (facing page bottom). Another of Kyoto's fabulous landmarks, and also considered one of Japan's most famous sights, the stunning Kinkakuji Temple, or Golden Pavilion (overleaf), was originally built as a retirement villa for Shogun Ashikaga Yoshimitsu and was later converted to a temple.

The Japanese calendar contains numerous festivals that take place throughout the year, many unique to a particular city or shrine, or linked to the changing seasons. One of Kyoto's three main events is the Jidai Matsuri, or Festival of Eras (above), which is held at the end of October to commemorate the founding of the town in 794. It is celebrated with a long procession through the city, involving over 2,000 participants dressed in historical costume. An annual event of a different kind is the traditional archery contest (facing page) that takes place at the Sanjusangendo, or "Hall of Thirty-three Bays."

Reputed to be one of the most beautiful cities in the world, different aspects of Kyoto (these pages) are emphasized by the changing seasons. Facing page: pedestrians stroll amid the stunning scenery created by snow- and blossom-laden trees, both in the Shinnyodo Temple area (top) and along the Path of Philosophy (bottom). Of equal splendor are the brilliant fall-colored trees, their glowing hues decorating the areas around the temples of Shinnyodo (above) and Kiyomizu (overleaf).

The grounds surrounding Manshuin (above) and Sanzenin (facing page bottom) temples, and lovely Senbon Shakado Park (overleaf), are all fine examples of the delightful gardens (facing page top) that flourish in Kyoto. Located in Kyoto's northern suburb of Ohara, the grounds of Sanzenin Temple are particularly admired for their lovely maples, verdant moss, and glowing fall colors.

Regarded as the most spectacular of Japan's fortresses, Himeji's majestic castle (left), known as the "White Egret," dominates the small town of Himeji. The present building dates from 1580, although the original structure was built some 250 years earlier by Toyotomi Hideyoshi, subsequently passing to his rival, Ikeda Terumasa, and then to over 400 different lords. A popular day trip from Kyoto, this well-fortified structure consists of a striking five-storied donjon, or keep, surrounded by three smaller donjons, moats and defensive walls.

Second only to Tokyo in economic and industrial importance, Osaka (these pages), also known as the "City of Merchants," has a long history as an influential center for trade, and remains one of Japan's major ports. The city can be divided into two main parts, Minami, the more unpretentious section, and Umeda, or Kita (these pages), the more industrial area in the north, comprised of towering high-rises and numerous stylish shopping areas. A major landmark in the city, the Sony building (above) indicates the site of one of the city's major shopping streets, the covered Shinsaibashi, where ancient shops stand alongside modern boutiques.

Captured at twilight, dazzling city lights vie for attention in Osaka (left), adding glamor to the looming skyscrapers and tingeing the waters of one of the city's few remaining canals (overleaf). Once referred to as the "City of Water" due to its numerous rivers and waterways, much of the network of canals that played such a crucial part in Osaka's commercial past has now been turned into roadways.

Acclaimed as one of Japan's most photographed sights, the famous floating Itsukushima-Jinja Shrine (right and overleaf) was constructed in 593 and forms the religious focal point of Miya-jima Island. Located near Hiroshima, amid the Inland Sea, this beautiful and sacred island is considered – along with Matsushima and Amanohashidate – as one of Japan's three great scenic attractions. Last page: bamboo is a common sight around many Japanese homes, providing, with its strength and flexibility, a useful building material.

INDEX